W9-AYO-221

HOLLAND

Designed by
DAVID GIBBON

Produced by
TED SMART

CRESCENT

INTRODUCTION

There is an old Dutch saying which claims that 'God created all the earth except Holland, which was created by the Dutch' and the creation or rather, reclamation of this low-lying land, a large proportion of which is well below sea level, has been no easy task. Its very name Holland (literally Hollow Land) accurately reflects the country's character. Not unlike a piece of jigsaw puzzle, the irregular outline of the Netherlands encloses some 15,892 square miles of exceptionally flat land, of which approximately 3,000 square miles have been laboriously wrested from the sea. Recorded reclamation dates back as far as the 12th century and ever since Holland's earliest days, the Dutch people have been engaged in a ceaseless struggle against nature and the disasters brought about by the constant threat of the North Sea. History has shown that this threat can never be disregarded. In 1421 for example, during the famous 'Saint Elizabeth's Night', the sea destroyed 72 villages in the Maas estuary and thousands of people were drowned; the flooded land called Biesbos (Reed Thicket) has never been reclaimed. Again in 1570 the 'All Saints' Tide' devastated several regions and even in modern times when really extensive reclamation schemes have been initiated, disastrous floods have repeatedly proved the insuperable power of nature. In 1953, the last of these devastating tides submerged 160,000 hectares, 1,800 people were drowned and 30,000 houses were destroyed or damaged. In recent years much of what was the Zuiderzee, the great tongue of water which formerly ate into the country from the north, has been turned into polderland, land surrounded by dikes and artificially drained but the Dutch remember that disaster is ever imminent and claim with a note of stoicism that 'the making of Holland is never finished'.

So many years of conflict with the sea have contributed not only to Dutch literature which abounds in legends associated with the mysterious quality of the ocean but also to the general character of the Dutch people. Their attitude is primarily one of common sense and realism and there are those who have seen their calm, methodical approach to life as stubborn and lacking in interest. Yet the Dutch are also possessed of a strongly independent driving spirit. Citizens of the 16th and 17th centuries rose time and again against foreign domination to found and secure their own republic and Dutch merchant ships sailed the world and so helped to lay the foundations of a great trading nation characterized by a vigorous spirit of enterprise. In the field of art, the history of painting would hardly be complete without including, beside those of Van Gogh and Rembrandt, the names of the other great Dutch painters: Jan van Eyck, the founder of the Flemish school in the 15th century; the allegorical Hieronymous Bosch in the 16th; the 17th-century still-life artists such as Willem Heda; and the geometrically inclined Piet Mondrian in the 20th.

Interest in art is still widespread. There are 32 state-supported museums in the nation, of which the Rijksmuseum in Amsterdam with its magnificent collection of the works of Rembrandt van Rijn is possibly the most famous. The modern creative spirit is by no means confined to the visual arts however. The Netherlands today has a vigorous economy, for the losses due to war and to the great flood of 1953 have been made good. Industry in particular, is developing rapidly, Dutch farm produce and cheeses are renowned throughout the world and large areas are devoted to flower growing, especially in 'Bulbland' which lies between the Hague and Haarlem. From here millions of hyacinth and tulip bulbs are exported every year. Above all, however, Holland includes the estuaries of the rivers Scheldt, Maas and Rhine and through their seaports the Dutch today control a large proportion of the world's water traffic.

Holland's capital, Amsterdam, despite its many ancient gabled buildings, which still as in Rembrandt's day overlook the shifting waters of the canals, is a bustling twentieth century metropolis. The famous 17th-century Mint Tower, built on the ruins of a medieval keep, now presides over a congested traffic intersection and perhaps here more than anywhere else the spirit of independence has found its expression, for Amsterdam is one of the liveliest centres of the international counter-culture of Western youth.

All this may perhaps seem a far cry from the traditional image of Holland and phlegmatic Dutch composure, yet some of the traditional images associated with Holland have been retained…and in some cases carefully nurtured. The neat, brick-built little towns, the magnificent colours of the spring tulip fields and the windmills, which for centuries have stood guard over the canals and polderlands, are still part of that characteristic Dutch landscape which appears in so many art masterpieces. Regional costumes and clogs are still worn; in some places they emerge only on special or festive occasions but in others, particularly in parts of Zeeland, they are still everyday dress. Traditional customs too, have been preserved. When a funeral passes a windmill, in many instances, especially in the Zaan valley, the miller will still stop it and put the blades in the recognised position of mourning: the face of the windmill follows the funeral procession across the country until finally the funeral passes out of sight. At times of great festivity on the other hand, the mills may still be specially decorated, their vanes hung with garlands, baskets or hearts. It is scenes such as these that have combined to make Holland the model of the small-scale masterpiece and a country where in the words of Sadi de Gorter, "the cities are threaded like pearls on the silver cord of canals and rivers, adorning eternally youthful green lands."

Illuminated by a string of electric lights, a bridge *left* spans the Herengracht at its point of intersection with the Reguliersgracht in Amsterdam.

Amsterdam's network of waterways, which during the 17th century enabled freight to be transported by barge to all parts of the sea-trading city, has retained much of its original atmosphere. A transport barge *above* makes its way through old Amsterdam and canals such as the Herengracht *below right* or the Waals Eilandsgracht *below* are still lined as *left* with characteristic narrow houses crowned with graceful gables. On a façade near the city centre *centre right,* an unknown artist has brought life to a blank wall by painting in windows and the Westerkirk offers a rare bird's-eye view of the tree-lined canals *above right.*

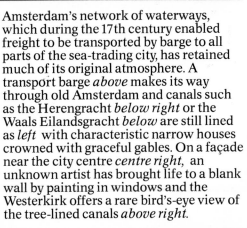

Trams *below right* or pleasure craft *above* moored in Damrak Harbour provide a relaxing means of viewing Amsterdam's many historic buildings. The wooden drawbridge of the Magere Brug (Slender Bridge) *below left* was constructed almost 300 years ago and is still raised by hand, and the Muntplein *below* and *above right*, one of the main traffic intersections, derives its name from the Mint Tower where the town coinage used to be cut. The building was constructed in 1620, by Hendrick de Keyser, on the ruins of a 15th century keep.

From the very edge of the Oude Shans rises the solid imposing construction of the Montelbaans Tower *above left and overleaf.*

The fascination of Amsterdam must surely
lie in its infinite variety...ranging from
the fashionably Bohemian atmosphere of
the Rembrandtsplein *above left,* the
exclusive restaurants and shops of the
Leidseplein *below left* and the busy whirl
of the fairground *below right,* to the quiet
dignity of St Nicolaas Kerk *above* and the
seclusion of the city's parks *below.* The
canals possess a life of their own and many
houseboats have all the conveniences of a
modern home *centre right.*
Bicycles too are a common sight in
Amsterdam *above right.* They are
particularly suited to its gentle gradients
and narrow, congested streets and hold a
special appeal for one of the world's most
pollution-conscious cities.

In North Amsterdam, the Zaanse Schans Living Museum *centre left* includes a collection of wooden buildings brought from different parts of Holland and restored. Among them, the polder windmill *above left* is typical of the mills used to dry out lands reclaimed from the sea in the north and west of the country. Volendam *above, below left* and *right* is a small fishing hamlet with a picturesque harbour alive with fishing boats. Hoorn *below* has also preserved its historical appearance. Its pretty façades, stylish houses and spice warehouses recall the town's significant role at the time of the East Indies Company.

At the Keukenhof Flower Exhibition *on these pages, previous pages and overleaf,* a splendid estate has been turned into an exhibition park of bulb plants. Here, beside picturesque ponds, among impeccably laid-out lawns, tulips, daffodils, hyacinths and countless other flowers form a blaze of carefully arranged colours.

Among the Keukenhof Gardens' artistically arranged flower-beds are over 700 varieties of tulips, the flower for which Holland is renowned throughout the world.

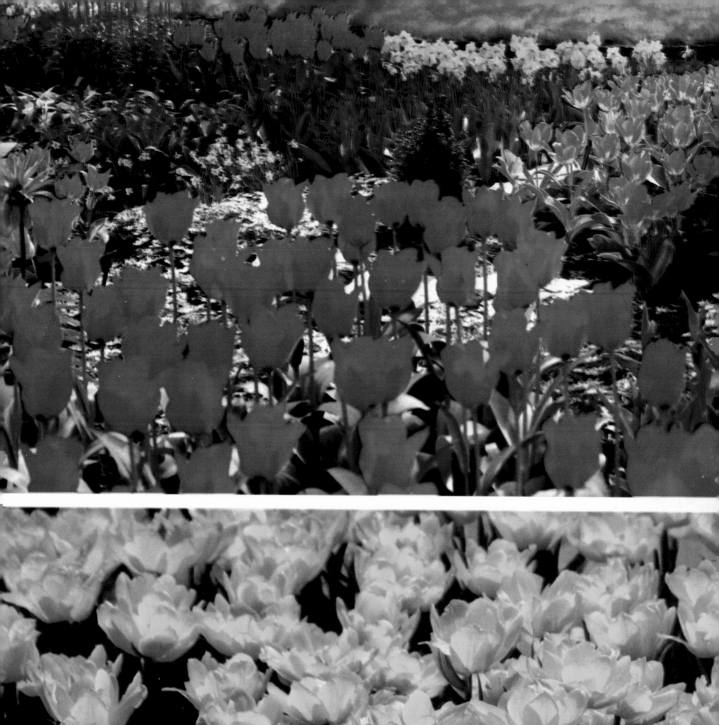

Housed in the Peperhuis, which stands on the Wierdijk overlooking the sea at Enkhuizen, the Zuiderzee Museum recalls the traditions and the life-style of a bygone era. Built as a pepper warehouse in 1625, the Peperhuis provides an appropriate setting for a fascinating collection of items and momentoes associated with what was once the Zuiderzee.

The Zuiderzee today is divided into the Ijsselmeer and the Waddenzee by a dam, the Afsluitdijk, which provides a magnificent view *left* across the waters it separates. Medemblik *above* is a picturesque old town on the former Zuiderzee, which was founded in 1288 by Floris V Count of Holland, on the site of the old Frisian city said to date from AD 334. Fields of flowers *right* surround Julianadorp, a village established in the centre of the Koegras polder and north of Alkmaar a windmill *below* rises in graceful silhouette against the evening sky.

On a cheese farm at Katwoude near Volendam, a husband and wife team work to make a variety of cheeses in the moulds shown *above left and below*. Here at the Jacobs Hoeve they produce some of the smallest cheeses in Holland.

Held every Friday morning, from the end of April to the end of September, the cheese market at Alkmaar *on these pages and overleaf* is conducted in strict accordance with a tradition of 300 years standing. Cheeses are brought to the market by barge and the round balls, weighing anything from 4-14 pounds, are pitched from the barge into barrows which closely resemble stretchers. They are handled almost exclusively by carriers wearing distinctive straw hats, which identify them as members of an ancient guild, who are entitled to transport the cheeses. The sale is conducted in a ring and finalized by a handclasp which is as binding as any written contract.

Marken *on these pages* is famous for its picturesque painted wooden houses, with roofs tarred and covered with tiles. In a wooden hut set in the middle of a car park, Mart Leek carries on a clog-making business handed down to him by his father and grandfather, using traditional tools, some of which are more than 100 years old.

In the flower-growing region near Lisse *above and below left* and *right* the spring-time landscape is a mass of brilliantly coloured tulips. Many of Holland's cities have retained much of the atmosphere of their historic past. Alkmaar *above right* is famous for its heroic defeat of the occupying Spaniards in 1573 and Haarlem's narrow streets and gabled houses *above* recall the days when this was the home of the Counts of Holland. The Cathedral of St Bavo in Haarlem *below,* with its beautiful cedar wood vault, was built between the end of the 14th and the beginning of the 16th century.

The small port of Monnickendam *below right,* with its lovely old houses, some of which date back to the 16th and 17th centuries, is renowned today for its smoked herrings.

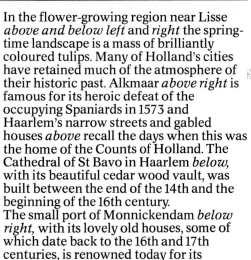

On every side of the town of Hillegom there are vast flower fields and the Year of the Child is celebrated *on these pages and overleaf* with colourful parades and giant floats made with meticulous care from thousands of the most beautiful blooms.

bloemenverkoop t.b.v.

NOORDWIJK helpt

BOVEN-VOLTA

The Hague *above,* seat of the Dutch government and parliament, is the administrative and political centre of the Netherlands. Its Peace Palace *above right,* designed by Cordonniek in Flemish Renaissance style, stands at the starting point of an avenue leading to the port of Scheveningen, which with its illuminated pier *left* has become the city's 'seaside resort'.

Utrecht, because of its central position, is known as the 'pivot' of Holland and its busy shopping centre *right and below right* is renowned for its trade fairs.

Tilburg *above and below* is a busy industrial centre and its streets, deserted by night, are some of the country's most congested by day.

Underneath Valkenburg lie a series of caves *left,* which were formed due to the extraction of building stone, begun some 2,000 years ago. In contrast to them, the Evoluon in Eindhoven *right* provides a glimpse of an ultra-modern world. Constructed in the shape of a flying saucer and housing a permanent exhibition of science and technology, this fascinating building was erected in 1966 to mark the 75th anniversary of the foundation of the Philips electrical company.

Market-day brings an additional array of food and flowers to the already enticing streets and shops of Maastricht *on these pages and overleaf,* and at the very centre of the crowded market stands the Stadhuis (Town Hall) *below.* Characteristically Dutch with its attractive carillon, this imposing building was completed in 1684 by the architect, Pieter Post.

To many, Holland is symbolized by the windmills which may be seen on the polders and dykes throughout the country: *left* in Groot Ammers, *below left* in the Openlucht Museum in Arnhem and *above left and below* on the polders near Kinderdijk (Children's Dyke) so-named because according to legend a cradle containing a crying baby and a mewing cat were washed ashore here in the flood of St Elizabeth, 1421. A view inside a windmill *above* provides a glimpse of its highly effective mechanism.

In an idyllic setting *right*, the Kröller-Müller State Museum in Arnhem has assembled a priceless collection of modern sculpture.

On the Baarn road in Soestdijk stands the Royal Palace *above left*, the residence of Queen Juliana and her family. Founded in the 17th century as a hunting lodge, the palace has an elegant white façade, flanked by two wings and is set among immaculate lawns, surrounded by beautiful woodland.

On the occasion of the birthday of Queen Juliana, seen *left* waving to the crowd, the Dutch people flock to Soestdijk in their thousands.

In costumes and colours representing the different regions, customs and activities of Holland, Queen Juliana's subjects file past in spectacular array as a demonstration of affection for their monarch.

Shipbuilding flourishes near Groningen *above left* where small vessels are built for inland and coastal navigation and east of Coevorden there are large deposits of oil. Near the old village of Schoonebeek a sinister line of pumps *left* loom above some 240 wells, to produce a daily output of 18,000 barrels.

The oceanarium at Hardewijk *on this page* provides a fascinating exhibition of killer whales, walruses, seals and dolphins, trained to perform the most spectacular feats.

Giethoorn *on these pages,* known as Holland's 'Little Venice' is a picturesque village whose houses and farms are accessible only by water. All transport is carried out by flat-bottomed boats and the houses form small islands, surrounded by greenery and linked with one another by miniature bridges spanning the canals.

Harlingen *above, left and below*, founded in the 12th century, today has a busy but picturesque harbour, connected with the Frisian islands and by canal, with Leeuwarden.

Menkemaborg Castle in Uithuizen *above right* is typical of the manorial homes of the country nobility. It stands in a moat, surrounded by a magnificent park *right* and its interior is furnished throughout in period style.

A Friesland windmill *overleaf left* stands reflected in the almost motionless waters of a canal near Workum.

Sheep graze with their lambs in fields near Marssum *overleaf right*.

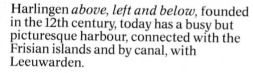

Potpa Castle, Marssum *left and above* was built between 1511 and 1525 by the powerful Heringa family. It subsequently became the property of Dr Popta, who housed his magnificent collections here and is now owned by a charitable foundation established by Dr Popta next to the castle.

A traditional flat-bottomed sailing boat, specially designed to draw the minimum amount of water so that it can be used on the canals as well as at sea, enters Stavoren harbour *below.* Another sailing boat, more modern in design, prepares to moor *right* and pleasure craft *above right* lie at their moorings in Oudega near Sneek.

A canal wends its way undisturbed through the market town of Leeuwarden *below right.*

First published in Great Britain 1979 by Colour Library International Ltd.
© Illustrations: Colour Library International (U.S.A.) Ltd, 163 East 64th Street, New York 10021.
Colour separations by La Cromolito, Milan, Italy.
Display and filmsetting by Focus Photoset, London, England.
Printed and bound by SAGDOS, Brugherio (MI), Milan, Italy.
Published by Crescent Books, a division of Crown Publishers Inc.
Library of Congress Catalogue Card No. 79-51714
CRESCENT 1979